History's Warriors

GLADIATORS

GAIL TERP

BLACK
RABBIT
BOOKS

Bolt is published by Black Rabbit Books
P.O. Box 3263, Mankato, Minnesota, 56002.
www.blackrabbitbooks.com
Copyright © 2020 Black Rabbit Books

Marysa Storm, editor; Grant Gould, designer;
Omay Ayres, photo researcher

Names: Terp, Gail, 1951- author.
Title: Gladiators / by Gail Terp.
Description: Mankato, Minnesota : Bolt is published by Black Rabbit
Books, [2020] | Series: Bolt. History's Warriors | Includes bibliographical
references and index. | Audience: Ages: 9-12. | Audience: Grades: 4 to 6.
Identifiers: LCCN 2018008466 (print) | LCCN 2018010251 (ebook) |
ISBN 9781680728552 (e-book) | ISBN 9781680728491 (library binding) |
ISBN 9781644660409 (paperback)
Subjects: LCSH: Gladiators–Juvenile literature.
Classification: LCC GV35 (ebook) | LCC GV35 .T47 2020 (print) |
DDC 796.80937–dc23
LC record available at https://lccn.loc.gov/2018008466

Printed in the United States. 1/19

Image Credits

Alamy: Heritage Image Partnership
Ltd, 6–7; The History Collection, 24; The
Print Collector, 28–29 (area image); avforums.
com: Casimir Harlow, 26–27; dinosauriens.info: An-
gus McBride, 12 (top); foto-basa.com: 4u2ges, 9; iStock:
bwzenith, 22–23; ilbusca, 12 (btm); Valerie Loiseleux, 31;
yuran-78, 32; mariafresa.net: XAVIER VALDERAS, 16–17 (gladiators); miguelcoimbra.com/: MiguelCoimbra, 18 (large image);
peterbullartstudio.co.uk/: Peter Bull Art Studio, 4–5; Shutterstock:
Andrey_Kuzmin, 28–29 (shields); Andrey Yurlov, Cover (bkgd);
A-R-T, 25; Dmytro Zinkevych, Cover (gladiator); Flipser, 14;
Ioan Florin Cnejevici, 23; Luis Louro, 3, 10–11; Maxx-Studio,
1; ms. Octopus, 16–17 (bkgd); Robert Adrian Hillman, 18
(silhouette); stmed.net: Unknown, 21;tributeandtriumphs.
org: Tribute and Triumphs, 15
Every effort has been made to contact copyright
holders for material reproduced in this book. Any
omissions will be rectified in subsequent
printings if notice is given to the
publisher.

CONTENTS

CHAPTER 1

Meet the GLADIATORS

Two gladiators enter the **arena**. They walk across the blood-soaked sand. The men raise their weapons. The crowd cheers loudly. One fighter has a sword. A helmet and shield protect him. The other has a net, **trident**, and dagger. Only a shoulder guard protects him. The men are well-trained. They're ready to battle.

5

The Crowd Decides

The two men fight with **fury**. They trade powerful blows. Then the swordsman becomes trapped in the net and falls. He can't escape.

He lifts his finger to show he surrenders. Now, the crowd decides his fate. "Kill him!" they roar. The emperor signals "Kill." The standing gladiator gives the death blow.

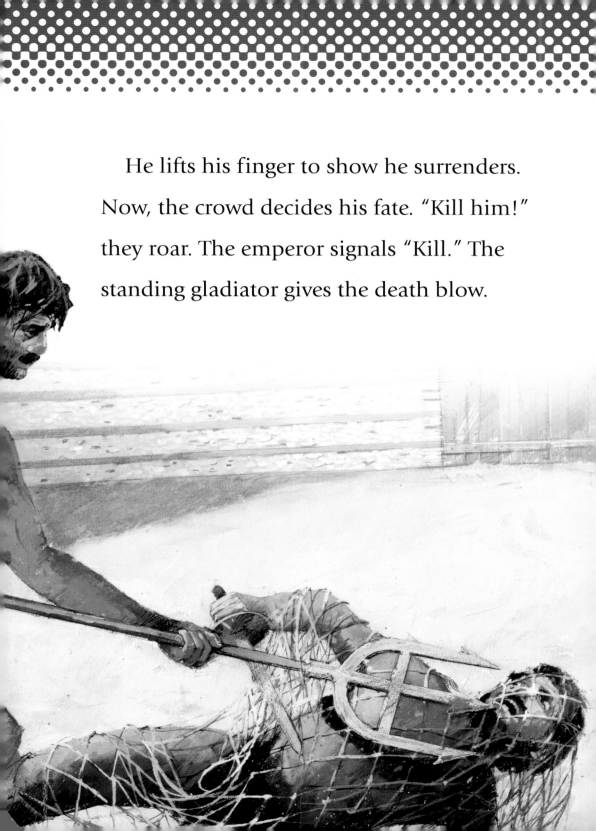

A Violent Time

Gladiators were **ancient** Roman warriors. They didn't fight against enemy soldiers, though. They fought against each other as entertainment. Winners received money and **glory**.

Gladiator fights began in 264 BC. At first, they happened at funerals. Later, leaders used them to **impress** people. Big, showy games were a sign of power.

The fighters were Roman superstars. The more they won, the more people loved them.

9

THE ROMAN EMPIRE

Ancient Romans lived in the Roman Empire. Romans controlled parts of what's now Europe, Asia, and Northern Africa. Their control lasted from about 27 BC to 476 AD.

ROME

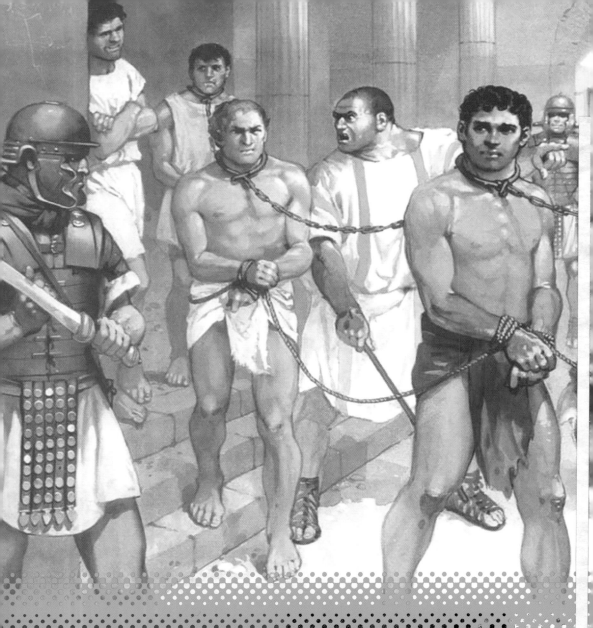

When fighters
got hurt, doctors
treated them.

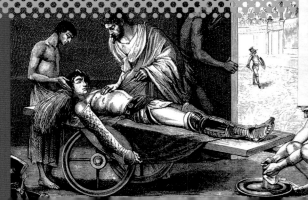

CHAPTER 2

Gladiator

Most gladiators were slaves or prisoners forced to fight. But some people volunteered. They wanted to become heroes and win money. A few women even fought. They battled against other women.

Fighters usually lived at schools. They slept, ate, and trained there. They shared meals with people they might someday kill.

Gladiator Training

Managers ran the gladiator schools. They worked with trainers to make sure the fighters became skilled and powerful. Each gladiator trained in one type of fighting. While training, students fought each other. They used wooden weapons. They didn't want to get hurt before the big fights.

Some gladiators could earn their freedom. Freed fighters sometimes became trainers.

TYPES OF GLADIATORS

Each type of fighter had its own armor. They also used different weapons.

helmet

armguard

helmet

small shield

curved sword

sword

large shield

leg guards

leg guard

thraex

murmillo

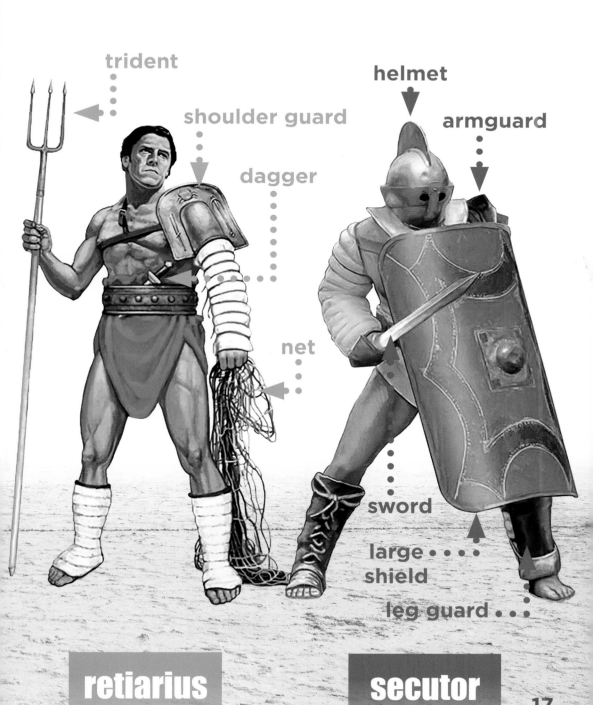

trident

helmet

armguard

shoulder guard

dagger

net

sword

large
shield

leg guard

retiarius

secutor

17

Game Day Schedule

TIME OF DAY	EVENT
morning	animal events
noontime	executions
afternoon	gladiator fights

CHAPTER 3

Gladiators in

Games were big events. They lasted all day with many shows. Morning shows involved animals, such as lions and tigers. Crowds watched people hunt the animals. They also watched the animals kill prisoners. During lunchtime, executions took place. Big gladiator fights happened in the afternoon.

Brutal Battles

Large crowds gathered to watch the big fights. During them, gladiators often fought against different types of fighters.

Not all battles ended with death. Sometimes fighters surrendered. Training a gladiator took time and money. Managers wanted fighters to survive. Then, they could fight again.

A slave named Spartacus became a famous gladiator. In 73 BC, he escaped from his school with other fighters. As they traveled, men joined them. They fought against the Romans.

BY THE NUMBERS

The Roman Colosseum was the largest arena. Many fights took place within its walls.

ABOUT
157 feet
(48 meters)
TALL

4
STORIES

22

**about
45,000
SEATS**

**80
ENTRANCES**

**TRAP DOORS
36**

**how long it took
to build**

**ABOUT
10
YEARS**

23

Emperor
Honorius

CHAPTER 4

THE END of Gladiator Games

The end of gladiators began in the late 300s. Games were becoming too expensive. People spoke out against them too. They said the killing was wrong. In 399, Emperor Honorius closed the schools. He later **banned** the fights.

Most gladiators fought a few times a year. They trained the rest of the time.

Gladiators Today

Gladiators may no longer exist. But their stories live on. Many movies and TV shows feature the fighters. Millions of people visit the Colosseum every year too. Gladiator fights are a thing of the past. But they haven't been forgotten.

TIMELINE

264 BC
The first games take place.

73–71 BC
Spartacus escapes and leads uprising.

about 70 AD
People begin building the Colosseum.

80 AD
The Colosseum opens.

399 AD
Honorius closes the schools.

404 AD
Honorius outlaws fights.

GLOSSARY

ancient (AYN-shunt)—from a long time ago

arena (uh-REE-nuh)—an area for competition or other activities

ban (BAYN)—to forbid by law

execution (ek-si-KYOO-shuhn)—the act of killing someone especially as punishment for a crime

fury (FYOOR-ee)—wild and dangerous force

glory (GLAWR-ee)—public praise, honor, and fame

impress (im-PRES)—to gain interest or admiration

trident (TRI-duhnt)—a spear with three points

BOOKS

Bodden, Valerie. *Gladiators.* Fighters. Mankato, MN: Creative Education, Creative Paperbacks, 2018.

O'Connor, Jim. *Where Is the Colosseum?* Where Is … ? New York: Grosset & Dunlap, an Imprint of Penguin Random House, 2017.

West, David. *Lots of Things You Want to Know about Gladiators … And Some You Don't!* Lots of Things You Want to Know About. Mankato, MN: Smart Apple Media, 2016.

WEBSITES

10 Facts about the Colosseum!
www.natgeokids.com/au/discover/history/romans/colosseum/#!/register

Ancient Rome: The Arena and Entertainment
www.ducksters.com/history/ancient_roman_arena_entertainment.php

Gladiators
www.dkfindout.com/us/history/ancient-rome/gladiators/

INDEX